Artwords

"In *Artwords*, Charles Ghigna paints in verse, offering poetic portraits of iconic artists and writers that are variously (and sometimes simultaneously) playful, poignant, and profound. Readers will relish these 'speaking likenesses,' which both pay homage to their subjects and evoke their most beloved artistic and literary achievements."

—**GRAHAM C. BOETTCHER**
Director, Birmingham Museum of Art

"The masters of paintbrush and pen come to life as Charles Ghigna uses poetry to capture the nature of their art while sharing a glimpse into their hearts. The resulting poems in this collection are exquisite yet accessible. While educational and informative, laced with biographical detail and fact, Ghigna's poems to the masters are, themselves, little masterpieces."

—**ALLAN WOLF**
Author of *The Snow Fell Three Graves Deep*

"Using a variety of poetic forms, Ghigna creates expressive poem portraits of two dozen famous artists and poets, from Claude Monet ('Bearded lover of light') to Walt Whitman ('A fearless wild phoebe'), bringing each one to life with witty allusions to their works and clever homages to their legacies."

—**DR. SYLVIA VARDELL**
Professor, Texas Woman's University,
and poetry anthologist, *A World Full of Poems*

"This may be Ghigna's best work yet."

—**DAVID L. HARRISON**
Author and poet

"Each of Charles Ghigna's twenty-four art-portrait poems is a masterpiece comparable to the famed artists and poets he apostrophizes in various magnetic poetic forms—Vincent Van Gogh, El Greco, Pablo Picasso, Walt Whitman, and Mark Strand, to name a few. Indeed, this is a book to put under your pillow at night so the craft and joy of it will inform the day."

—**SUE WALKER**
Professor emerita, the University of South Alabama, and former Poet Laureate of Alabama

"Written with admiration and deep understanding, these poems by Charles Ghigna bring us into direct contact with the creative process of twelve poets and twelve painters. By addressing the artists who have influenced him, Ghigna engages intimately with the sparks of brilliance they emit and helps us remember, as he writes in 'El Greco,' that the greatest art is about 'more / than meets the eye.' After reading these lyrically rich poems, I felt inspired to revisit my own beloveds."

—**JENNIFER HORNE**
Poet Laureate of Alabama

Artwords

Artists & Poets: Portraits in Verse

Charles Ghigna

RESOURCE *Publications* · Eugene, Oregon

ARTWORDS
Artists & Poets: Portraits in Verse

Copyright © 2021 Charles Ghigna. All rights reserved. Except for brief quotations in critical publications or reviews, no part of this book may be reproduced in any manner without prior written permission from the publisher. Write: Permissions, Wipf and Stock Publishers, 199 W. 8th Ave., Suite 3, Eugene, OR 97401.

Resource Publications
An Imprint of Wipf and Stock Publishers
199 W. 8th Ave., Suite 3
Eugene, OR 97401

www.wipfandstock.com

PAPERBACK ISBN: 978-1-6667-0384-9
HARDCOVER ISBN: 978-1-6667-0385-6
EBOOK ISBN: 978-1-6667-0386-3

07/27/21

*for Charlotte and Christopher,
makers of words into art*

*for Chip Ghigna,
poet with a paint brush*

*for Debra,
always*

A*rtwords* is a series of twenty-four portrait poems, each written as a personal letter to the artists in the literary form known as the apostrophe, an open letter. The portraits present a variety of poetic forms ranging from free verse to traditional forms such as the villanelle. Each form was chosen to best portray the life and style of their artist.

Contents

~ *The Artists* ~

Claude Monet | 3
Edgar Degas | 5
Henri de Toulouse-Lautrec | 7
Henri Matisse | 9
Mary Cassatt | 11
Edouard Manet | 13
El Greco | 15
Vincent Van Gogh | 17
Pablo Picasso | 19
Jackson Pollock | 21
Georgia O'Keeffe | 23
Andrew Wyeth | 25

~ *The Poets* ~

Robert Hayden | 29
Ezra Pound | 31
Dylan Thomas | 33
Emily Dickinson | 35
W. H. Auden | 37
John Berryman | 39
Sylvia Plath | 41
Anne Sexton | 43
Mark Strand | 45
Robert Frost | 47
Carl Sandburg | 49
Walt Whitman | 51

~ The Artists ~

Everyone discusses my art and pretends to understand,
as if it were necessary to understand,
when it is simply necessary to love.

Claude Monet
1840–926

Claude Monet

Bearded lover of light,
you braved the sun and snow
to follow her Giverny glow
through the clouds, the crowds,
the pools of water lily,
to capture her on canvas,
to have your way with this
most perfect model *plein air*.
"When it gets dark," you said,
"I feel as though I'm dying."
And we thank you here
for staying alive,
for brushing your brilliance
into our eyes
with such a touch
of everlasting light.

Art is not what you see, but what you make others see.
Edgar Degas
1834–1917

Edgar Degas

Perfectionist with a paint brush,
you taught your eyes to see off-center,
your fresh angles freeing you to view
space and form with new focus.
Uniting classical with experimental,
your soft images jockeyed and danced
across paper and canvas
in charcoal, oil, and pastel,
growing more vivid and abstract
with each turn until at last
you brushed your friends away
and filled your final days
with dancers and horses
made of clay.

Painting and sleeping—that's all there is.
HENRI DE TOULOUSE-LAUTREC
1864–1901

Henri de Toulouse-Lautrec

Although the critics were unkind
To your gaudy, bold design,
Your brash and brilliant, new display
Of every Montmartre cabaret
Would set the stage for imitation
Of all your poster innovation.
The orange hair, the garish light,
Each graphic scene set to excite.
A draftsman of debauchery,
You painted pain's frivolity.
And though your life was cut in half,
Your work lives on, a loud last laugh.

Creativity takes courage.
HENRI MATISSE
1869–1954

Henri Matisse

The conductor
of a silent symphony,
you led your imagined lines
through scores of movements
until the sculpted air
could hold its breath no more,
until the patient canvas
begged for your baton
to brush the mute melody
into the imagery of tone
that echoes still from the eye
of their maestro, medium, magician
of paper, pen, and pencil,
of scissors, knife, and hand,
of color, line, and air.

Acceptance, under someone else's terms, is worse than rejection.
MARY CASSATT
1844–1926

Mary Cassatt

From Philly to France
(against your father's wishes),
you left your impression
upon the Impressionists.
Degas' hand-picked protégée,
you painted maternal rings around
the fraternal masters,
etching and earning
your way past the best of them,
your sense of style and grace
painted upon each pensive face
still stares through the eyes
of your immortal mothers
and all their fatherless children.

There is only one true thing: instantly paint what you see.
When you've got it, you've got it. When you haven't, you begin again.
All the rest is humbug.
Edouard Manet
1832–1883

Edouard Manet

Most poetic
of the first
modern painters,
you brushed aside
the accepted notion
that a narrative
of pretty pictures
makes art.
Free from story
and moral,
you dared paint
for painting's sake,
each stroke,
a new beginning
with never an end
in sight.

I paint because the spirits whisper madly inside my head.
El Greco
1541–1614

El Greco

A Spaniard from Greece
who mastered the Italian
technique of chiaroscuro,
you planted a landscape
whose hills still sow hope
in the hearts of artists
who follow in the deep
shadows of your footsteps,
praying they, too,
might brush against
that fine line between
the natural and supernatural,
might escape, as you did,
from material truth and form
to rise and enter that kingdom
where light and dark
are but a door to more
than meets the eye.

I dream of painting and then I paint my dream.
VINCENT VAN GOGH
1853–1890

Vincent Van Gogh

You saw beyond the blue that filled your eye
And like a child lost in evening prayer,
You brushed against the stars as you passed by.

You spun nocturnal truths out of the sky
In waves of rolling flame upon the air.
You saw beyond the blue that filled your eye.

Your steeple still transcends the hills that try
To touch the golden dreams that held you there.
You brushed against the stars as you passed by.

You searched the other side where shadows lie
In swirling pools of night upon your stare.
You saw beyond the blue that filled your eye.

But Theo and Gachet could only try
To pull you from the depths of your own glare.
You brushed against the stars as you passed by.

Your final stroke fell on a canvas sky
Where dreams once prayed upon the evening air.
You saw beyond the blue that filled your eye.
You brushed against the stars as you passed by.

Art is a lie that makes us realize the truth.
Pablo Picasso
1881–1973

Pablo Picasso

You carried your world in a cubist cage.
You painted its bars with passion and rage.

And when you were lonely with nothing to do,
You stripped all the bars and painted them blue.

Hanging your soul for the life of your sister
In memory's museum to show how you missed her,

You painted Conchita, the Devil, and Christ,
Your trinity set for one blessed price.

You painted and paid for your premature guilt
Till your reds and your greens grew into a quilt

Of beggars and clowns and self-portraits, too,
All without color, except bitter blue.

Your fragmented world was coming undone
And painting to you was no longer fun.

So you crawled in your cage and pulled it apart
And beat it all back with a broken heart.

And when your rage had painted you,
Your cubist cage was finally through.

Painting is self-discovery. Every good artist paints what he is.
JACKSON POLLOCK
1912–1956

Jackson Pollock

Reclusive spider,
you spun your
abstract web
of expressive splashes,
spills and drips
around the world
until in a swirl
of genius rage
you reached the end
of your last thread,
climbed into
the car-wreck corner
of your self-made madness,
and left us all
a palette of perception
that still spins
before our eyes.

I decided that if I could paint that flower in a huge scale, you could not ignore its beauty.

Georgia O'Keeffe
1887–1986

Georgia O'Keeffe

Like the baby's sky
that lives beyond
the gentle touch of truth,
your pastels rise softer
than a daylight dream.

Your golden eyes
belong to the stars
of another world
where shade and shape and hue
of yellow, purple, blue
unfurl like calla lilies
in a field of lilac.

In warm, blending tones
of sleeping summer babies,
you showed us how to wake
our eyes to the meaning
and motion of light.

One's art goes as far and as deep as one's love goes.
Andrew Wyeth
1917–2009

Andrew Wyeth

You are the back of the attic mirror.
From your side we see only out.
The change of seasons you sketched
leaves a reflection on us all.
You wear your silver fleck in pieces
like the holey No Hunting sign
aired by the bully's bullets.
The wind whistles through, not at, you.

We speeding faces fly by your painted past
searching for a glimpse of the still town,
for the attic barn draped in shadows,
for the unfinished spider's web,
for the opened door, the paneless window,
for the field where Christina lies,
for the chance to look through Helga's eyes
and to see, just once, more than there is to see.

~ The Poets ~

*Art is not escape, but a way of finding order in chaos,
a way of confronting life.*

ROBERT HAYDEN
1913–1980

Robert Hayden

You said poetry unites us,
transcends all that divides us,
saves us from ourselves and each other,
chases darkness from its corners,
becomes the guiding star
that shows us who we are.
You said poetry is the exaltation
of the things that keep us alive,
like a father no one thanked
who rose in the dark from his bed
on winter Sunday mornings
to start the fire and polish
his son's good shoes for church.
You said poems are like that,
like little unseen angels
who wear the wings of our best souls.
May your poems, Dear Robert,
continue to rise and shine
like your father and the shoes
he polished with love for you.

Great literature is simply language charged with meaning to the utmost possible degree.

EZRA POUND
1885–1972

Ezra Pound

Oh most modern
of the Moderns,
editing Eliot
out of his waste land,
disabstracting Yeats
from his metaphysics,
resurrecting Frost
from his death
of the hired man,
showing Joyce
how to milk the moocow
and lead him up
Black Mountain,
you came down
to take the Metro
to Mauberley,
the Cantos all the way
to *tout le monde.*

Do not go gentle into that good night.
Rage, rage against the dying of the light.

DYLAN THOMAS
1914–1953

Dylan Thomas

You rose like a comet
from your dad's deathbed,
your words searing into
a sudden villanelle of stars
that shone like diamonds
brighter than the fire
of your burning eyes,
but it was your voice,
your soaring voice,
that held the sun.

Hope is the thing with feathers.
EMILY DICKINSON
1830–1886

Emily Dickinson

Stanza upon stanza
your elegant extravaganza
of poem upon unpublished poem

came to life upon your death
gave birth and endless breath
to your world made new.

Dear Amherst Belle
may your spell
ring true.

*A poet is, before anything else,
a person who is passionately in love with language.*

W. H. AUDEN
1907–1973

W. H. Auden

Lionized and Pulitzerized,
you entered your self-imposed cage
with the wrinkled face

of a tired truck driver
climbing out of a whisky dream
to take his place behind the wheel,

your elegant haul of words
roaring their way
down the open road.

One must be ruthless with one's own writing or someone else will be.
JOHN BERRYMAN
1914–1972

John Berryman

You marched into the gray eyes of dawn
feeling older than the bones
that held their ground
like grazing, aged cattle
waiting, eyes closed to the wind,
on a winter, slaughter morning.
You searched through the fog for a sign,
but there was no sun to burn the way,
no burst of rainbow bridge
to keep you from the cattle call.

Poetry is a tyrannical discipline.
Sylvia Plath
1932–1963

Sylvia Plath

Inside the silent Bell Jar,
you sat on the kitchen floor
playing "Mother" as a child,
talking to your dolls like children,
cradling your kittens like babies—
until the night of the real mother play.
You lay open and swollen on the table,
straining to hear the first cry,
the white masks floating above you
while the scalpel did its work
to keep you from splitting in half,
the bare, white room spinning in silence,
spinning in silence, still.

When writing, I know I'm doing the thing I was born to do.
ANNE SEXTON
1928–1974

Anne Sexton

In a bouquet of memory,
you confessed
your final thorns,
pinned them all to paper,
your red dress falling
like a petal from a rose.

If every government official spent an hour a day reading poetry, we'd live in a much more humane and decent world.

MARK STRAND
1934–2014

Mark Strand

In a church
You were the absence
of church.

This was
always
the case.

Wherever you were
You were
what was missing.

When you walked
you parted
the sacred air

and always
the blessed air
moved in

to fill
the spaces
where your body had been.

We all
have reasons
for moving.

You moved
to keep things
holy.

I have never started a poem yet whose end I knew.
Writing a poem is discovering.

ROBERT FROST
1874–1963

Robert Frost

Your soft words
fall like fresh snow,
blank white verse
upon the countryside
of our heart,
fill the forest
of our dreams
with hills of light
that silently lead us
through the trees
back to our own
endless road
not taken.

Poetry is an echo, asking a shadow to dance.
CARL SANDBURG
1878–1967

Carl Sandburg

You said you searched for syllables
to break through the barriers
of the unknown and unknowable,
to speak of and for and by the people
of America and your city of Chicago,
of its harbor and railroads and steel,
of its fog and grass and greed,
of its children and hobos and poets,
of its fighters and huskers and friends,
of its Saccos and Lincolns and Sundays.

We thank you here for all your iron words,
for forging them past the softer landscapes,
beyond the hush of poetic sunsets
into the brutal roar of the city
where you told the truth on us,
on all the dusty faces and places of America.

I sound my barbaric yawp over the roofs of the world.

WALT WHITMAN
1819–1892

Walt Whitman

A fearless wild phoebe,
you still fly up and down
our country's spine
trying to find the sun.
Your tickles tell us we must *live*,
must chase our hours into corners
and hang them in gold cages
whose bars are far enough apart
for flying things that love escape.
You tell us we must exercise
our right to fly beyond
this time of day and night,
must stretch to touch our toes,
must bend our rainbow backs for birds,
must straighten up and set them free,
must watch them soar, and follow.

www.ingramcontent.com/pod-product-compliance
Lightning Source LLC
Chambersburg PA
CBHW060430050426
42449CB00009B/2231